ASK THE WIND

VAGABOND
VENICE/CULVER CITY, CA

ASK THE WIND

Selected and New Poems

Mahnaz Badihian

VAGABOND

editor@vagabondbooks.net

Published by VAGABOND
Mark Lipman, editor

VAGABOND

Intellectual Property
Badihian, Mahnaz
Ask the Wind
1st ed. / p.cm.

ISBN13: 978-1-936293-48-3
Made in the USA.

To a world void of wars and hunger.
To human rights and freedom of speech.

"The morning wind spreads its fresh smell. We must get up and take that in, that wind that lets us live. Breathe before it's gone."

~ *Rumi*

TABLE OF CONTENTS

TRIBUTE TO SPRING

I feel so ripe
as if I were just born
from a tall tree in the garden.
Fresh leaves spurting all over my skin.

I cannot stop growing
every second under the
the clear whistle of sunshine
on this Sunday, before spring.

I feel so ripe
as if coming out of
the winter ground
carrying with me a taste
of many springs.

Is it me, or the aroma of
the coming spring or the
recycling of love in my heart
which helps me with rebirth
So beautifully today

Ask the Wind

OUR KISSES

We kissed under the bombs
in our homeland
under the thunder of fear and doubt
We kissed
on the streets of diasporas
on the roads of despair
in the city of the devil

We kissed so much
that our lips joined the eternity
under all the beliefs
under fire and blood
under executioner's sword
under distorted news

We kissed quietly
our kisses had a different color every day
Sad kisses
love kisses
kisses of excitement
kisses of fear
kisses of death
friendship kisses

our kisses were talking
when they silenced our voices
and our lips became our safe heaven!

Mahnaz Badihian

ASK THE WIND

I can share my love
with wind
with roses
with thorns
with dying daffodils

I ask the wind, will you blow my kisses
to the other side of the river,
to fresh weeping willows gazing timidly
to the one waiting for me
hoping the distance becomes shorter

NOT BELONGING

Like a bird, she floats in nature
like water, she seeps through the earth
the cells in her body,
do not identify with anyone
she is everyone

She has no motherland
she's free from friends and enemies
the recycled woman rises to far horizons
with no destinations in mind

She'll not be wounded, not be sad
she's free of old memories,
from belonging to one particular land
from heavy gold necklaces
her ancestors left behind

Now she puts her feet on fresh grass
opens her arms and lets the sun plant
flowers on her fingertips

Gives her naked bosom to the hands
of the breeze under the glory of
the apple trees
giving herself to the flowing creeks
letting the fish swim in her veins
for the birth of more new happiness.

Mahnaz Badihian

IMAGINE

Imagine that every morning on every door
A stem of a flower, of love, hangs
void of locks, chains, and iron fences.
And every day on the streets,
children play like free birds.
Hand in hand with full bellies
with the right shoes on their feet
going to school,
without fear of being stolen.

Dogs and cats like dear citizens,
walk with patient men and women

We can imagine that we all can
live together
without war and bloodshed,
Wherein people shall worship
the earth and the lands.

A world in which every human death
would be a disaster.
And in it, there will be fruits,
and trees and plants,
in place of cannons and guns,
anthem and poetry in place of
anger and hostility

YOUR SHIRT

I came back, and the smell of
your body floating in the room

The purple shirt you left behind
looking at me and has the look
of your caressing hands

You left your undershirt behind and
I forgot to take the history book with you

In these voiceless hours
you're staring at me through
the purple shirt still holding
the warmth of your body in it
and the perfume of your imaginary
presence is intoxicating

Mahnaz Badihian

ROAD

If I could become a road
soft and gentle,
for you to walk on, I would
if you could carry love
on your shoulders
on this very rough road!

OCEAN

The day I was riding
on the ferry from San Francisco,
I saw someone was walking
on the surface of the ocean
who was dead years ago.

The ocean we love,
with its endless beauty, had a chest
filled with drama, screaming
with the echoing voices of the dead,
and the wounds of unfortunate sailors
and the melody of the corps of migrating birds.

While each new wave
was swallowing the previous wave,
the ocean had a gift for the forgotten dead.

The gift of blood on its shores,
The gift of the lifeless body
of the little boy, Artin Iran-Nejad
with a piece of his mother's dress in his fist.

The gift of a lost pair of shoes
arriving with each wave
from unknown rivers and oceans

I felt the burning of the ocean's heart from
black oil dripping on its blue chest from tankers
from the black boxes drowned with
the destiny of countless lovers.

Mahnaz Badihian

Sitting in the ferry on that foggy morning
towards San Quentin
where the body of my friend,
Fay was found years ago.

From the window,
I looked at grayish, restless water
and saw that Fay's eyes were repeating
in thousands,
on the chest of the Pacific Ocean,
in a circular motion

Her long hair has covered
the surface of the cold water
trying to be a nest for the lost birds

I stretch my hands to grab her
from the threshold of death
but she was disappearing, hand in hand with
with hundreds of people who lost their last breath
in the Pacific Ocean!
I lost a friend and her image in the same water.

LATE NIGHT

Late night,
In the cold weather
of November in San Francisco
I was walking between tents
Placed next to each other
not too far from the luxury stores
in the Business district

Stores that sell one t-shirt for the price of a
week's food for a low-income family
Perfume shops and handbag sellers,
Jewelers with an item more expensive than
tuition for a semester of college

As I was getting close to the occupiers
I felt the confidence,
and the strength of the people.

Occupiers sat in a group
Playing, singing, dancing, chanting,
all calm and peaceful
A few drinking coffees or eating food
A few selling books
A few working on an occupy logo
And all preparing for the
Long road ahead

Mahnaz Badihian

I AM STILL A CHILD

As if years and days were asleep
I'm still that little child
that loves her lacy shoes,
and her errant hair
that hardly reaches her shoulders.

As if years and days were asleep
and my hands still are
those of a child,
demanding another hand
to jump over a creek,
and my childish heart
gets confused by the
first encounter with love.

What happened to all those years,
have I lost the experience of
living in this strange world.
I'm still a child in my mother's eyes,
who never left this house.

Come and see this child.
She has tamed the years,
and the moon engulfed
in her childish palms.

YOU ARE BEAUTIFUL

My daughter was beautiful
next to the mirror of Dorian Gray
under the moon.

There was something
in the locks of her hair
more surprising than
the turns of history.

And the moon with a mythical shadow
escaped from the vineyard
hiding in the corner of her lips.

I told my daughter:
You're aware, with a conscious mind.
You're on the verge of saving me,
and save the one who thinks
we will seize life from malice one day.
And divide the remainder of our pride.

One day we will fly our milk-filled breasts
under the Sun for the thirsty birds.
So, they can build their nest
on the top of our breast.

My daughter knows
she's beautiful in her mind.

Mahnaz Badihian

Beautiful are her mighty hands,
she knows very well that the roses
dry in gardens every day, every year
for only the roots can stay.

I said to my daughter,
"You're beautiful."

So beautiful that with the daughters
of unknown lands, with prairie girls,
with homeless and hungry girls
together you will all divide the Sun
on your shoulders to teach us equality!

Returning from Lahore trip to San Francisco, 2008.

DNA

It was Monday morning and
I was passing the big statue
In the lobby of Johns Hopkins hospital
searching for Room 202,
the first interview with Mrs. Willis

She had a kind smile on her lips
her hands were wrinkled with red nail polish
Mrs. Willis looked me in the eyes,
how do I pronounce your name, dear?
I said, MAH NAZ,
the exact same way it's written

Mrs. Willis with her M.S. degree said, I'll try
MENAZ Manos, Maha-noss
then gently she changed her voice and
said, Can I call you Mary?

Marry? Merry? Morry? Echoed in my head
I felt like evaporating morning dew,
like a branch of a tree under heavy rain,
like fruit just fallen from a tree

I looked Mrs. Willis in the eyes and said,
"But my name is the charm of the moon
the name I was called by my mother
and by the man with black hair
dark mustache and brown eyes."

Mrs. Willis was looking at me
with wide- open eyes
I said: "Mrs. Willis,
is my name more difficult
than Deoxyribonucleic acid?"

Mahnaz Badihian

MR. VICI

Apart from problems,
Wars and savagery
Caused by human beings
The new little dog, Mr. Vici
Has occupied my heart
And left no room for anyone

Mr. Vici kisses me
He puts his head on my arms,
If he hears a stranger breathing
Behind my door
He barks heroically
And with innocent eyes
He tells me, "I love you."

Strangely, I believe in Mr. Vici
The little dog who understands
The language of love
I need this love

WALL

What is it about the walls?
Used to be a place we could
hide behind as a kid
a place we exchanged
our forbidden kisses
with the one we loved.

A wall in my childhood memory
that I watched
the sunrise on its shoulder
and sunset on its skirt

As I got older,
the walls showed me
a different meaning
The wall they bombed
and poured on poor people's heads
a wall they built to stop human interaction

We then demolished the Berlin Wall
and enjoying the Hadrian Wall
built by Roman Emperors
while Enclave of Melilla fed
to the sorrow of Moroccans
knowing Moscow once died
behind the Kremlin Wall

Mahnaz Badihian

We are all invisible walls
my accent is a wall
your words are a wall
our beliefs are a wall.

we are builders of walls
wall of selfishness
wall of racism
wall of poverty
wall of alienation

Walls smell of crime,
blood, poverty, and separation!
Let's ruin the walls before they're built

SILENCE

This colorful silence
knows me, and always
waits for my arrival.
the land of silence gravitating
to forgotten memories

BULLETS ARE FORGETFUL

How many winters need to die,
for one spring to come to life?

What has the firing squad done to
fresh dreams that abruptly
the greens turned to red corpses

Who will pick up the shattered dignity of
the families who have undergone
rape and rage in the hands of criminals

It is the dark we need to be aware of,
when criminals wake up to steal
our dream and the share of our bread
while the ever-sleeping God
closes his eyes and ears to
these wounds, wars, cries

But the bullets are forgetful
and keeps returning to the
same people everywhere
simple working people

Nothing left in this unjust World
to hang on to, except our dignity

For Afghan workers

LET'S DREAM KINDLY

The room was filled with
lost dreams.
Music was from captured humans
in the battle for humanity

They are still hopeful angels
busy making headless babies
with human hearts.
with the manuscript for pre-fabricated
head wrapped in their umbilical cord.

This room is where Adam and Eve
based their first fertile egg and a bird
flew to eternity with broken wings,
with two legs that only walk through
a limited plane of a little universe

Let's dream kindly!
While the moon is still looking at us
And our incredible silenced pain
heals with tuned music of hope.
Let's stop making headless babies
With short hands.
We will make remote-controlled wings
for every dreamer to rise!

Mahnaz Badihian

EXCHANGE

All the kisses we exchange
every day with ones we love
all the hates and pains we endure
all the sickness and disease
disappears with us after a while
because humans vanish every day
to recycle again and again to a new us
with the art of new kisses and new hates

LIFE

What if our life was tasteful
bright, and beautiful
like a pomegranate
we could live next to each other
nicely, like pomegranate seeds

Mahnaz Badihian

I WAS THERE

Witness to a human being's insanity
Killing, demolishing, and beheading
I was there
And the news of wars
Hungry children
Rape
Fear of police
Fear of losing your home
Fear of capitalism
Hit me in the head every single day

I wished the world was my baby
And I could cuddle it
To feed it and protect it
A baby that could grow in nature
With peace
Next to flowers and trees
Birds and animals

Let us start this World over again
Let's call Adam and Eve
to make kinder, gentler babies!

Utopia or Dystopia

One day when someone
waters our gardens on time
feeds our birds for us
while making chicken soup for all
and lets me know where to go,
when to go and how much to pay
for a stem of red rose for you.
when that someone possibly
will choose a friend that
fits my emotional needs

That someone is not Cyrus the great
which will hand opportunities to all
it is not the messiah who will love all
it will be a robot with artificial intelligence
who simply can make educated decisions
and will understand infinity better than us
and will be void of hate, anger,
jealousy and affections
will have more wisdom than Rumi
and more knowledge than
Aristotle and Razi combined,
but it will not be significant as dinosaurs
or small as a dragonfly

And that is the day we will
become classic animals and
think and act differently
we will be a numb being
which follows the orders
of his creation
while hoping for a life
without wars and hunger

A.I. will divide all foods
evenly between us and
has no race preference
A.I. will horde our knowledge
hold the keys to our houses
and walk freely in our bedrooms
measure the intensity of moonlight
and romance between stars

Let's see if A.I. will kill us all
or create a utopia.
Too soon to judge!

Ask the Wind

WHAT FEAR

They always scared us of poverty.
Now what's left to be scared of,
we're all getting poor together.

They always scared us about breaking laws.
What fear,
they broke all the laws in front of our eyes
and the world was witnessing

They scared us of homelessness.
What now,
we're all becoming homeless
whether by wars or banks
or even by loss of our jobs.

They scared us with blood and death every day.
What fear,
we see blood and killing
and terror in our media everyday
and we're used to seeing the killing
and bombing everywhere

They scared us over the left, becoming the right
and the right becoming the left.
What now
that neither left nor right
can solve this vast human misery.
Now our only fear should be separation,
separation of our hands and hearts,
separation of our voices.

Mahnaz Badihian

DRY RIVER

In my hometown Isfahan
the river was dry

People would walk
around it and sing
songs of despair

The entire river bed
was covered with
hollow stories of the past

The magical music
and dance of water
was what people
imagined in their heads
instead of this absence

What things they stole
from us...

River, bread, freedom

WEEPING WILLOW

Who wrote the genuine poems,
those in contact with gods of love
those who know of suffering
those who experienced still waters
and witnessed dying buds
on the vast universe

Those who like José Marti
knew of life in captivity
and next to his cell
tall trees have rooted
those who in the hallucination
and their imagination
can see shadows and dark days

Those who with the warmth of their heart
can warm up our lives
those who under the flog of dictators
had a lot to say with their poems
those who walked through rugged roads
and recognized the light
at the far end of the tunnel
and their heart experienced
blood and daggers

Those who have secret talks
with roots of evergreens
and those of weeping willows
who wrote the genuine poems

Mahnaz Badihian

SOLA

Open your suitcase Sola
Life started with this journey
to immigrant camps.

Sun is shining; spread the memories
on the greenery of grass, to evaporate.

Get up. Spring is on its way
and the weary horses of winter
are dancing with steps of spring.

Spread your hair
upon your tired shoulders,
hold your head up
so your childhood tears
dry on your face,
so the parasite of grief disappears
on your tired skin.

Give a new meaning to life,
away from the betrayal of the lovers.

Redefine love,
the love that sings a fresh melody
and brings you into the garden
through the gate of caressing.

Ask the Wind

Make sense of freedom
to get rid of the influx of parasites
from the vulture's point of view
from the dagger of false verses.

The evergreens are standing next to you
and hope has thrown a carpet
at the extent of desire
with your great courage.

Step on the misery.
Open your suitcase to the rainbow at dawn
along the peaks of patience.

*For Sola, a woman who learned to breathe in the dark and
cold weather, surviving immigration camps, in the hope of
reaching bright horizons,*

INTOXICATED GOD

Fill your cups with Shiraz.
Raise your cups to the weary God,
deep-rooted and ancient.

Sprinkle water from the springs
on the God to wake up after centuries,
ignoring this world in rage.

We want an intoxicated God
a happy and elated Lord of Hope
with a commandment of bliss.

Dance toe-to-toe.
Dandelions are dancing.
Good news arrived,
the sun is shining bright
and the intoxicated God
stopped commanding war and carnage,
stopped ordering crime and famine
and will stop commanding
volcanoes and tsunamis.

Intoxicated God
laughs, dances
and fills human cups
with eternal wine.

GOD SPEAKS ALL LANGUAGES

I wake up every morning,
noticing the wars found
their way to my bedroom

I wake up, seeing the war
is a blanket on my bed
with the picture of grieving
mothers in my head,
the same grieving as when my mother
lost her son in the old war

While asleep, my hands
are searching for the lost
limbs of children in the ruins
and making shelters for
the families in the war-stricken lands

Every night a poem
about war-ridden countries
and its hungry children sleep next to me

We're all thirsty
for freshwater from rivers
that smell of basil and daffodils

We need kind sleeves to wipe the tears
from the faces of homeless kids,
the eternal losers of wars

Mahnaz Badihian

All the tornados are not enough
to blow away the flaming sorrow
in the heart of mothers
who lost their children to the war

The blood of all the kids
who died in Gaza, Yemen,
or elsewhere have a voice.
The corpses of all the innocent
people who died
have courage for revenge,
because it's adding up,
because the imaginary God
speaks all languages

CONFUSION

If you decide to forgive me
I'll make it easy for you
I'll tell you how for so long
I was trapped in my soul

And how I was lost
in the confusion of exile that
I couldn't hold those weary
moments calm and clear

If you decide to forgive me
for not being there by you
side by side, day by day
let me tell you about the time
I was lost, facing a strange direction

Can I forgive you for being absent
in those tough days that I needed
caressing hands and a loving soul

Mahnaz Badihian

THEY'RE NOT MATILDA AND NERUDA

That was the story of their generation
women would suffer in marriage
day by day and never think of divorce

My parents, not precisely hating each other,
not exactly in love, lived together
feeling apart for so long
finally, in middle age, mother chose exile
apart from her husband and far from
the two pomegranate trees in her garden

But separation ended at the end
when in the graveyard, they slept
head to toe about each other
Indeed, they're not Matilda and Neruda
lying down next to each other in Isla Negra
but I like this closeness in the graveyard
I have only to say "I love you" once

Wondering if at night when they're alone
they can catch up with some practice
on the subject of love.

Ask the Wind

TEN YEARS AGO

I dislike this night
when people are temporarily dead
and the creaking of walls is alive
the antique china bowls
with red roses on them still smells
of fresh yogurt and cucumber
made by my ancestors

The old handmade mattress was there
with faded sunflowers on it which one day
held the body of my bird in it

My companion, the moon with its gaze
as long as the shadow of Alborz Mountain
creeps in through the windows
landing on my memories

Right here, behind this curtain
is the station of memory
with an old plastic bag
that holds many old letters
from the station of exile
with the handwriting of father
on love letters, boys wrote to me
when I was a teenager

I dislike these long nights
with fat, swollen roaches
finding a moment to look at my face
especially on the same street
that my bird died ten years ago

Mahnaz Badihian

WAKE UP

Oh, you lazy, wake up
the sun is out
pour your kisses on me
let my laughter shine
in your black eyes
and the night gets lost
under the enamel of your teeth

Night is over
and I am picking the last stars
from the strands of your hair

Rose Garden

Leaving behind the dead and elderly
Leaving behind their roses

Their life was thrown in a tiny suitcase
escaping the ruins of the motherland
hoping to stay alive by escaping
streets and burned cities

This poem is for you, Alan Kurdi
Your small lifeless body on the shore
burned our heart

What happened to all the birds
Why are the evergreens broken
What happened to the rose garden
Why is Damascus an orphan now
The eyes of Aleppo are taken out
Palmyra lost its hair to darkness

All you wanted, Alan, was a piece of bread
without blood and a bullet on it
All you desired was an inch of Sun
without gunfire
You wanted a vegetable garden
without body parts

Mahnaz Badihian

I want to be a safe road you take
I want to be a cup of milk you drink
a piece of bread for your empty stomach

I want to be a strong cradle
to carry you safely to the shore
I wish I was shoes on your feet
to walk you to a safe nest

*For Alan Kurdi (a little boy from Syria who died
while escaping the war zone) and all refugees*

TEMPLE OF SOLITUDE

My mother was not too rich
but she paid for all my travels
to the land of dreams
She never forbade me from going
to the late-night parties with stars

With her generosity
white butterflies would be let free
on my skirt for my birthday

But my father was more generous
he let me get drunk
with the beauty of grapevines
while my drunken brawl
would bring reconciliation between
poplar trees and evergreens

My father was so open-minded
that he would allow me to travel
in my dreams to the end of this universe

Even the day I was in the temple of solitude
and my enemies tried to remove
the sunshine from my innocent shoulders
he stood by me and screamed:
"She is my God; I worship her."
That day was the beginning of my awakening
and believing in eternal love

Mahnaz Badihian

GODS IN KERALA

Here in South India
next to colorful fabrics,
the abundance of fresh baskets of petals
girls with beautiful black eyes,
people worshiping awaiting gods

With the smell of intoxicating
sandalwood and burning incense,
all hands are up towards all these gods
asking for something

Stores are filled with statues of gods
god of poetry
god of wealth
god of health
god of love
god of rain and light
god of everything and anything

And I am thinking with all these rose petals
in baskets and colorful bags,
and the aroma of perfumes
I must visit the gods

This is Kerala, "God's own house,"
and any statue you see
is a small god, a symbol of giving

Every day with a flower, I visit a god
One day visiting Krishna, god of love
another day visiting Lakshmi, god of wealth

Ask the Wind

One day I decided to visit poor neighborhoods,
old and ruined houses with a pile of
garbage next to broken doors
I looked at worn out and sad faces
of skinny dogs,
thirsty, hungry, and weary,
along with the fat and strong cows,
marching freely and happily on the streets

I see an old lady with a frail body
carrying a big load of wood on her back
barefooted men and women everywhere

Here in South India, I can see with my eyes
that all the gods are sitting and doing nothing.
the god of money has been sleeping for centuries
and did nothing in "God's own house."

For fun every day I buy
a statue of a god as a gift
for my wishful friends

Mahnaz Badihian

THE CRUEL ART

If I had the art of breaking hearts
I could break your heart
and use its pieces to mend mine
but I don't have the art of breaking hearts

I wish you were a bird
I would open windows for you to fly
to green lands, to Tamalpais Mountain
next to the Golden Gate

LUNAR WATER

From now on,
I'll only drink water from the moon
never again a sip of earthly waters
not from the bloody water of the Euphrates
or the Mississippi with thousands
of broken hearts floating on it
not water from the Ganges River
and its hundreds of worshipers

I'll go up there and fill my fists
with the water from the moon
then I'll pour it drop by drop
into the mouth of the thirsty
Zendeh river in the city of Esfahan
I'll water the arid garden in the parks

* *Zendeh Roud is a river in Esfahan, Iran, which is dry now!*

Mahnaz Badihian

TESTOSTERONE

Oh, if there was no war
my brother could come
to my daughter's wedding
and my mother would gift
her necklace to her

If the war did not happen
my son could read Hafiz
and would be free from
computer war games

If the war did not happen
I was still buying bread
in my mother tongue every day
and I would consult my aunt
about my female problems

But the war happened
and Pinochet broke
melodic hands of Victor Jara
and Shamlou was tormented
We all lost someone somewhere

War happened and
wars will happen because
testosterone is always alive!

MY EVERGREEN

This is my country too,
I buried my pomegranate tree here
my mother died here
and I raised my evergreens here

Mother liberty called for children
of other lands to gather here
This country needed the children
of Rumi, Hafiz, and Adonis
to enchant its land along with
the children who grew to be
Walt Whitman and Maya Angelou

Where were you when we came
with baskets of basil and poems,
with biblical fruits as a gift

This is our country too
we gave you our brightest brains
paved your soul with our art and culture

Fortunately, the universe
is our home the city of Isfahan
and the city of San Francisco too
I can call Isla Negra my home
where I visited Pablo Neruda's grave
next to his house
next to the resting place of Matilda

Mahnaz Badihian

Because human hope
art and poetry are universal
because we are all children of this planet
with or without hotels

I could not be happier than
to see all hands united
in celebrating freedom and peace

We are the children of Zoroaster
daughters of Moses and Mohammad
sons of poplar trees everywhere

You call us Muslim or Jew
you name us black or white
but we like to be called
a member of the human race

Mr. President, you can move us away
from the gardens we watered
for decades in this land
you can scare us with your
orders, but gardens are everywhere
the Sun shines everywhere
the moon belongs to everyone
with or without hotels

We will take our roses to the other side
of the river, to different continents
but you only have one home
your gold-plated prison
filled with intolerance and prejudice

Ask the Wind

MUSK DEER

We ran in search of you
on the soil, you lost your life
we never found an inch of your body!
but the soil smelled of evergreen
and daffodils from your youth

We filled our fists from
that aromatic soil mixed it
with Zayandeh Ruod water
and created a piece of art
as memorable as Persepolis

you became the river running
through our house
filled by our tears

You became a young Musk Deer
from Isfahan
the perfume of your skin
never left us

In memory of my missing brother in action

Mahnaz Badihian

COLD FIG

Through the windows of my bedroom
I heard your voice standing next to the garden
holding a big bowl of cold figs in your hand

Your voice was crispy when you said:
"Boy, it's chilly down there in the garden."
Then you added:
"But my lungs need this fresh air."

I asked you, can we have breakfast
looking at me with your beautiful eyes
you said: "Why don't I go out
and buy bread from the baker
while you're making the omelet."

The day was short,
and I enjoyed visiting my aunt
with you to deliver small gifts
I was happy because I only saw them
a few times in my life

We were still talking, but minutes later
I found myself next to your grave
on the outskirts of Isfahan

Have I missed something
between our breakfast that day
and your journey into the earth

STERN GROVE

San Francisco is cold in August
hundreds of people,
some old, some young
gathered in this grove,
sitting on blankets or folding chairs

Lying on the ground
underneath tall, old trees,
the smell of wet redwoods moving
through the breeze along with
the clear voices of opera singers
and the hands of a conductor moving
as if birds flying and dancing,
people holding a glass of wine, or coffee
The branches of trees are swaying
with the voice of the opera singer!

I want to be the wind at this moment
moving swiftly through the leaves
I want to be branches on top of the trees
I want to be the lyrics in their voices
or to be the dancing fingers of the pianist
so I can forget the sad news of our world

* Stern Grove musical festival is free and runs each
Sunday during the summer.

Mahnaz Badihian

I'LL LEND MY HANDS

Sometimes the only ones
I can talk to are my hands
I speak to my silent skin,
squeezing anger from my fingers

Sometimes we're the only two
who can understand the story
of life with no dialogue

I'll lend my hands and
the songs on my palm
to wandering kids
In alleys and streets

I know the day will come
when no bird will be starving
because the seeds of the helping
hands of Recycled women
will cover the entire plain

I Didn't Know

I didn't know how much I loved you
till I saw you shaving, fixing your tie
and waxing your shoes

I didn't know how much I loved you
till I saw your imperfect way of living
with the open buttons on your shirt
your off-center tie and your zipper
halfway open with your hair
almost always half combed

I didn't know how much
I loved you imperfectly!
but love is not always perfect
and I'm in love with you
so imperfectly every day!

SINCE YESTERDAY

Since yesterday there are
more decisions to make
it seems the wind blows
harder on our empty porch
Recycled woman feels the heaviness
of dead cells on her skin

Yesterday she was a few
hours younger
and a bit more careless
It's those yesterdays
we miss living
as they leave us with regret

COME BACK

Come back to this house
and pick up all this nothingness
we want you behind these windows
to wipe out shadows formed
in your absence

We want you to sit
around the dining table and tell us
about your challenges in life
since you were only fourteen
when you constantly
found and lost happiness
where you got to see first hand
hidden pain and the problems of others

Come back
we have time now
to listen, to love, and to have you
we'll leave the windows open
come back to our house

Mahnaz Badihian

DEATH

It's death
hiding everywhere
arriving at unknown houses
without permission

It's death ready
at intersections, behind doors
sometimes under the floral sheets

Death is standing in a simple suit
with iron cufflinks
or a golden cane
and a sharp eye
that stares randomly
Demise is covered in perfume

It's death, ready
carrying a handbag
filled with gun powder and bullets

Death is quiet
except for the moment he
passes through the red lights
with pride

Walking anonymously
with medals and honors
on his shoulder for yet
another unexpected catch!

Ask the Wind

PERFECT NIGHT

I suspect a night as perfect as tonight;
the purple floral curtain dancing
like drunken ballerinas
next to the painting of a lady
with a lacy red dress and scared eyes
with a gaping open mouth

I hear the frogs calling to each other
next to the morning glories
and the smell of abundance of hyacinths
touching the green sheets on my bed
where a man, like a naked statue, is sleeping

Next door, there is a room that I never knew of,
I hear mother's voice coming through it
and already forgetting that she lost her son,
her country, and her youth

Through the window, I also see the girl
who was shot on the streets of Tehran,
washing her face with the hose
blood pouring next to poplar trees

I only suspect a night as perfect as tonight
It's 2:00am, and I just discovered my legs

I never liked the darkness and the nights,
but I have to help the girl
next to the poplar trees tonight

Mahnaz Badihian

I am worried that I'll wake up the trees
and disturb the frogs and never find
the girl they shot on the streets of Tehran

Now, no longer could I hear the frogs
but I could feel the breeze on my green pillow
putting me to sleep in the early morning!

ESMAIL

I'm talking to you, Esmail
When was the last time you had
a sip from the Caspian Sea
for your dreams to come true

When was the last time,
your heavy shoulders
warmed up with happiness while
walking across Persepolis

Tell me, Esmail,
when was the last time,
your laughter splashed on your poems
On those cruel lonely days
did I see you quietly crying
walking across King's Cross
remembering your country
and the ones you left behind

Tell me, Esmail,
your heart couldn't tolerate life
without a cup-to-cup feast of drink
when you lost the things you loved

Where this road ends, Esmail
read me your longest poem
in the moments left to us.

Mahnaz Badihian

WHERE IS MY LOVER

Why my lover with his strong hands
was never born
and I lost the chance
to nap under his kind skin
amid lonely days

I have always dreamed
that my lover with his smiling eyes
filled with ghazals of Shiraz
and sweetness from Isfahan
from the alleys of calmness
slowly stepping into my ventricles!
with his breath smelling of daffodils
and his body filled with romance
asking me if I am happy
like the first flowers in spring
and suddenly, I feel like
a sugar cube is melting in my heart
knowing someone loves me tenderly

But where is my lover
maybe at the time of his birth
with a kick of a satanic man
he died in the blood of his mother
perhaps he was killed by tyrants
or by accident or war
or maybe he killed himself

Now every day
I come home with a bouquet of daffodils
for the sorrow of all the loves we lost

Ask the Wind

SOBHANEH*

While mother was in bed
and the morning dew still fresh
I lay in the quiet
curled under a comforter
listening to the rhythm of father's
movement around the house

I could hear the softness
of his black leather shoes
as he puts them on while holding
a white porcelain bowl with
red roses painted on each side
headed towards the big wooden door

The door opens with the familiar creak
and minutes later the same door,
the same noise as father returns with
the bowl filled with honey and butter
and the aroma of fresh bread called
Sangak** makes me leave the bed

Father pours water in the samovar,
lays a sofreh cloth over the Persian rug
and sets out the bowl and the bread
with a basket of fresh herbs

Mahnaz Badihian

He calls my mother's name
his voice is loud
soon he's sitting while eight hungry hands
dip Sangak in the bowl one by one

Now, after many years that he is gone
every day before sunrise, I see him
putting on his black leather shoes,
or coming back with a bowl in his hand
and a faint smile on his face

* *Breakfast*
** *Sangak is a special bread*

LAND TO LAND

I go,
from land to land
from this dream to another
something has been lost in me,
an audacity, a cause, a sense
but I do not find what I lost

Maybe I'm in search of
my childhood happiness
or the joy of walking
in alleys of the city of Isfahan

Maybe searching for
the loving gaze of pomegranate gardens

Whatever it is I am looking for
is not retrievable
not touchable
not visible
not possible
it's a feeling called nostalgia
that measures the length of our lives

Mahnaz Badihian

RAIN

It's the fourth day of heavy rain
the mirror I'm holding
shows deep lines on my forehead,
stretched lines around my lips

The rain managed to
curl up into my eyes

My love, can you go back
to the spring garden
pick fresh basil for lunch,
fresh hyacinth for the table

I was thinking to take a moon bath
letting the moon splash on my skin
with your voice like a soft velvet
caressing my face

I was thinking to hold life
In my arms lovingly
then the mirror falls on the grass

I soak my hands in the rain
and curl up my hair with rain
thinking life keeps walking so fast
that we don't notice fallen mirrors

Ask the Wind

RISE

Rise
to the senses of your rights
to the injustice you witness
it's not the slavery era with the mantra:
"Still tongue makes a wise head."

Sitting quietly
is the reason we lost the path
reason for still waters
and roads ending in dead ends
reason for having
tyrants, lunatics, criminals as leaders

Behind this short wall
underneath this old blanket
on this torn carpet
hands of many heroes grow strong

Do we remember the hands of
Frederic Douglas and Fidel,
have we read poems of Phyllis Whitley
kidnapped from West Africa and enslaved

Maybe the time has come for
"Lions to write history."

We can build pillars
beneath broken walls
under the fractured bodies
of poplar trees

Mahnaz Badihian

There's not a road
we can't walk down together
there's no final word
we can't say together
don't doubt that there's a hero
sitting, in each one of us
waiting to rise

Rise
we know there were people
on this graveled road
who reached green plains
to the vastness of mountains

There were people
who walked
with wounded feet
over rough roads
to be able to defeat
the most powerful criminals

Rise
"if I rise
If you rise
everyone will rise."*

One hand has no voice

* A line by Iranian poet Hamid Mosaddegh

CELEBRATING NOROUZ

We had to soak a bowl of wheat
and swaddle them in a
wet cloth for a week
then spread those sprouted grains
In a beautifully shaped dish
and let them grow
We'd make colored
figurines to represent us
sitting atop the wheat

Then mother would go
to "Charbagh" bazaar and buy
a few little redfish as a symbol of life

On the table we had hyacinth
to freshen the room
then came time to color eggs
mother never forgot to put
open-paged Hafiz on her chosen ghazal
while reciting the lines

She told us never sleep in old clothes
the night of Norouz

From day one to day twelve
we would visit every family and friend
On the 13th day of Norouz
we had to throw those planted grains
in any river we could see,
to have those old, sad roots
taken away from us

Mahnaz Badihian

HAFEZ

Where should I go tonight to find you
in this sunny Sunday of May
I feel silenced by your absence

There's no door that opens to you
there's no telephone that can
dial to your voice
and there's no city that hosts you
I'm even far from your graveyard
this is the art of exile!

Remember we sent your body *par avion*
to be buried in our motherland
We wanted those tall, big poplar trees
to grow from your dust, from your bones,
but there's always one thing that connects me
to you every day, a book by Hafez
and your handwriting on that page
where the poem reads:*

*The breath of the morning breeze will be aromatic
and this old universe will be young once more
The flower is so dear in this garden,
cherish it, as it will leave the garden very soon*

It's been ten years and I'm wondering
how tall the poplar trees are now
I close the page and imagine
a garden with a tall, green,
familiar poplar tree

*A verse by Hafez, translated by M.B.

THE LITTLE BOY

I read "little boy," and I cried
I cried for that little boy
and the bitter story of a child
who didn't see his father,
who didn't taste his mother's love,
but he created love and became a poet,
a painter, and an intellectual icon

The boy who became a pacifist
after seeing the Nagasaki horror

The boy, who was unwanted
and was shuffled from house to house,
from an orphanage to strange people,
and became the man
who made impossible possible.

The boy who experienced a rise
and fall of this world for a century,
and taught us that
we're getting older every day,
but our soul can stay young
and our minds can stay strong
if we keep life simple and flexible

Helping the rise of progressive
and radical voices, by defending
the poem Howl, and his book store became
the new intellectual hub of the Golden State

Mahnaz Badihian

He proved that to want is to be able.

Today he is that 102-year-old little boy,
who we lost weeks ago

We lost the Wings and Feathers
of poetry in the Golden city

The city which will always keep him alive
in the heart of its culture and literature

Keep watching, little boy,
Signature Ferlinghetti olive trees
in North Beach will grow taller

For Lawrance Ferlinghetti

Ask the Wind

THE 20s WON'T LEAVE ME

I was born on this day
in the vineyard
when father was intoxicated,
and mother was a cute goddess
the tree of my life has been flowering
for centuries, but the 20s won't leave me

The river of my body exhausts
in the waters of the world,
with the craze of the fish

The trees bloomed and died
Violets took lives and dried,
but the 20s won't leave me

Like the fig tree of the house
in the garden of San Rafael,
which had fresh figs sprout
from the dried-up branches

Like the tree in my childhood home
in which the four seasons were always alive,
but the 20s won't leave me

My childish heart
becomes joyous with a stem of flower
with crazy mystic music of Aref Ghazvini*
I grew taller under the cypress tree,
under the mulberry tree,
under the old pine tree,
in the neighborhoods of San Francisco

In the alley gardens of Isfahan,
next to the watercourses of my ancestors,
I stood tall as the height of time
but the 20s won't leave me

Something in my heart is alive and boiling,
alive like an almond blossom,
like a fresh spruce leaf,
like the sun at the peak
of Sahand and Sablan Mountain

Like the fish in the Atlantic Ocean,
alive like the dazzling light of my mother's eyes,
like the endurance of a fighter for freedom,
and the 20s won't leave me

* *Aref Ghazvini was a musician, and song writer of 20th century Iran.*

Ask the Wind

THIS DOOR

I'll close the door
Loneliness might arrive slowly
unaware of my soul
landing on the dew of my skin

Even with a tap on my door
I embrace silence hard
and I say to myself:
From this door,
friends and foes
bring with them
loneliness and trouble

I close the door tight

LIKE A NEW PLANT

I told memory to shut down
so like a new plant I can
ascend out of the ground
and my new me can forget the past

I'm a Recycled woman coming from
the earth of forgetfulness
I haven't read any verse,
any pieties
and here is this new terrain
in this neighborhood

No one ever stepped on me
No one ever buried the baby girls alive

I have obscured all the old meanings and laws
deep in the rebirth of the earth

FOR THE RED POET, JACK HIRSCHMAN

I feel closer to the galaxy today
soaking under rain
following the lost stars
with this news waking me up all night
with wonderous Arcane poems
chewing on my books

But can one believe
that the guiding voice of love leaves this earth,
while his footsteps are still alive in North Beach

Which part of this galaxy
has he landed in now
Maybe he flew to eternity,
to spread love from above

Who was this man
Tall, with the wild mustache,
with a heart as sensitive as a child's
and the energy of a young lion

Now that he won't walk around City Lights;
Now that he won't meet us in Caffè Trieste
and won't send us emails,
I think the end isn't too far for all of us.

How's it possible
to see the sun go down
right in the heart of summer
in the city of San Francisco

Mahnaz Badihian

The Red Poet
will never come
to my house again
to eat Persian food
and read Rumi with me

I'll complain to Rumi
I'll complain to Walt Whitman
for inviting Jack to eternity
only to have the Red Poet next to them

But let's remember to celebrate Jack
Let's dance behind house number 858A
Let's put red roses in Aggie's hair
celebrating the man we all adored.

BIPOLAR

I laugh then I cry for being in this world
I'm from the North
but my roots embedded in the South
I used to be Persian,
now I'm from the Iowa River
I listened to music in Shour and Beedad*
now the weeping of Yo-Yo Ma's finger
penetrates my heart

I used to read Rumi and Hafez
now I read Langston Hughes,
Neruda and de Anderade

I used to swear to love,
now I swear to life
I used to spare my life for others
now I think of me and us

I have two poles
one hidden, one you see

* Shour and Beedad are genres of Persian music.

Mahnaz Badihian

OH AZAR

It's a pity for you not to be here
and these cherry trees
get old without you

Was it you who picked up
a handful of cherries for the man who loved you
and now he's sleeping under the cedar tree

It's a pity you won't be here next season,
and the sunshine holds off its pleasant
warmth from your shoulder

You have a share of this farm
a share of the beauty of the cherry trees
with its opiate laughter

Stay alive so the cherry trees
bloom in this garden every year
You in your cheeky shirt
that sprinkles color on the earth

Oh, Azar,
it's a pity not to be in this cherry garden again
which will bloom with your memory forever

* *July 2019 In memory of Azar, who died from breast cancer*
months after a trip to a cherry farm

Ask the Wind

EARTH

lands, moon, and the Sun
are here to stay
and our eternal mother, Earth
will hold us in her arms forever
and will treat us all the same
solid, quiet, breathless

PUT YOUR SHOES ON

My love,
I saw you putting on your green shoes,
to join the people on the streets,
chanting for change

To change the scene on the streets
In this world with wealth and glory on one side
and tents on cold asphalts on the other

To change the way,
we divide everything:
Poor and Rich
Black and White
Ugly and Beautiful
Jews and Muslims
East and West

Go on, put your shoes on, my love.
It's time to put our shoes on,
to focus on our similarities
as human beings.

Focus on a piece of bread,
for all, with no blood on it.
To die from natural causes,
not by guns, bombs, and hate
on the streets of Chicago, Paris or Palmyra.

Ask the Wind

We may not achieve the change we want now,
but we can hope for a future
with new gardens without chemical dust,
with children growing with their families
without poverty and witnessing wars.

Keep putting on your shoes, my love.
Walk on the roads uniting our voices.
If not here, I will join you on another road,
somewhere in this World!

Mahnaz Badihian

ABOUT THE AUTHOR

Mahnaz Badihian's artistic expression started at a young age in elementary school by writing poetry and short stories and painting with whatever material was available. Life took her through many different experiences such as Nursing school, Dental school, art school, revolution, immigration, and motherhood, but she always remained a poet and artist. For 15 years now, her life has solely been dedicated to art and literature. She has published many poems and translation books in the Persian language and English. Mahnaz has been exhibiting her art internationally for decades, most recently with a solo exhibition in 2018 in San Francisco, California, at Live Worms Gallery. Her latest collection of poems, *Raven of Isfahan,* was published in 2019 to critical acclaim. Badihian finished her MFA in Poetry in 2007 from Pacific University in Oregon. Her poems appeared in more than ten international anthologies. In 2020 Mahnaz edited and published 300 pages of COVID poetry and art from around the world in a collection entitled *Plague 2020*. She is an active member of the Revolutionary Poets Brigade in San Francisco. Member of PEN, acting member of World Festival of Poetry. Her novel *Gohar* will be published in 2023.

VAGABOND